CW00665691

hat Women SAY

THE LITTLE POCKET BOOK OF

And What They REALLY MEAN

A humourous guide into the world of 'woman speak.'

BB

www.booksbyboxer.com

Published in the UK by
Books By Boxer, Leeds, LS13 4BS
© Books By Boxer 2016
All Rights Reserved

ISBN: 9781909732438

No Part of this publication may be reproduced or transmitted in any form
or by any means, electronic or mechanical, including photocopying,
recording or any information storage and retrieval system, or for the
source of ideas without written permission from the publisher.

Food & Diet

WHAT SHE SAYS

Pizza's fine

WHAT SHE REALLY MEANS

What an un-romantic skinflint!

WHAT SHE SAYS

I need the loo

WHAT SHE REALLY MEANS

I need to check
my phone

WHAT SHE SAYS

It's OK, I'll pay half

WHAT SHE REALLY MEANS

If he makes me pay half - that's it!

Food & Diet

WHAT SHE SAYS

I need the loo

WHAT SHE REALLY MEANS

I need to check
out if there's anyone I know in
this restaurant, and if there's
anyone I'd like to know

WHAT SHE SAYS

I'm hungry

WHAT SHE REALLY MEANS

I'm STARVING
and could easily eat the leftovers from the next table

Food & Diet

WHAT SHE SAYS

I'm not hungry...
really

WHAT SHE REALLY MEANS

I'm STARVING
but need to eat
less than you!

Food & Diet

WHAT SHE SAYS

Yes. The food was just right, just enough

WHAT SHE REALLY MEANS

I could eat that all over again, and more, but I can't appear to be greedy

Food & Diet

WHAT SHE SAYS

I feel absolutely fantastic on this new 5:2 diet!

WHAT SHE REALLY MEANS

Actually, I'm starving!

WHAT SHE SAYS

I`m on a diet
(in a restaurant)

WHAT SHE REALLY MEANS

I'll order rabbit food and you order something tasty and fattening - so we can share!

Food & Diet

WHAT SHE SAYS

I'm on a diet
(at home)

WHAT SHE REALLY MEANS

You will eat what I eat. Why should I suffer alone trying to make myself look good for you?

WHAT SHE SAYS

Let's go for a quick drink

WHAT SHE REALLY MEANS

I'm not coming home until I can't speak

Food & Diet

WHAT SHE SAYS

I've had a bottle of tropical fruit juice

WHAT SHE REALLY MEANS

I've had my 5-a-day

WHAT SHE SAYS

I'll just have a glass of wine

WHAT SHE REALLY MEANS

Wine is a liquid, those calories don't count

Food & Diet

WHAT SHE SAYS

Of course you can try some of mine

WHAT SHE REALLY MEANS

I mean a small bite, not all of it – and don't slobber while you do it

Food & Diet

WHAT SHE SAYS

My friend has been
advised to gain weigh

WHAT SHE REALLY MEANS

I now no longer
speak to her

Food & Diet

WHAT SHE SAYS

I'm full, I had a big salad for lunch

WHAT SHE REALLY MEANS

I'm freaking starving, so move that cake away from my face!

Food & Diet

WHAT SHE SAYS

It's Friday...
I'm allowed a treat

WHAT SHE REALLY MEANS

This treat is going
to be a feast!

WHAT SHE SAYS

I'll just have half a portion

WHAT SHE REALLY MEANS

I need to find the biggest portion possible

Food & Diet

WHAT SHE SAYS

I'll will only have
a couple

WHAT SHE REALLY MEANS

I'm going to eat the
whole, damn bag!

Food & Diet

WHAT SHE SAYS

I'm going to eat healthily all this week

WHAT SHE REALLY MEANS

It won't last past lunch time today

Food & Diet

WHAT SHE SAYS

Where has all the chocoalte gone?

WHAT SHE REALLY MEANS

If I deny it, then it never happened

Dating

Dating

WHAT SHE SAYS

I like you, but...

WHAT SHE REALLY MEANS

I DON'T like you

Dating

WHAT SHE SAYS

I don't want
a boyfriend

WHAT SHE REALLY MEANS

I don't want YOU
as a boyfriend

Dating

WHAT SHE SAYS

I need space

WHAT SHE REALLY MEANS

I need space - without you in it

Dating

WHAT SHE SAYS

Size doesn't matter

WHAT SHE REALLY MEANS

Unless I need
an orgasm

Dating

WHAT SHE SAYS

It's great being single

WHAT SHE REALLY MEANS

Oh my God! Life can't get any worse!

Dating

WHAT SHE SAYS

I love being single

WHAT SHE REALLY MEANS

I don't have to get out of bed and go to the bathroom to fart

Dating

WHAT SHE SAYS

I'm so happy for you both

(Speaking to her)

WHAT SHE REALLY MEANS

How can a bitch like you get a man like that!

Dating

WHAT SHE SAYS

I'm so happy for you both
(Speaking to him)

WHAT SHE REALLY MEANS

I hate you, and I hate your bitch!

Dating

WHAT SHE SAYS

I prefer the company of men

WHAT SHE REALLY MEANS

Other women hate me

Dating

WHAT SHE SAYS

Your friends are great

WHAT SHE REALLY MEANS

We'll get rid of them all - one by one

Dating

WHAT SHE SAYS

I can't do this week, how about next?

WHAT SHE REALLY MEANS

My diary is empty. I'm desperate. I have no social life, but I don't want to appear to eager

Dating

WHAT SHE SAYS

Isn't it amazing? They're engaged and they've been together less time than us

WHAT SHE REALLY MEANS

Christ! How much more of a hint does he need??

Dating

WHAT SHE SAYS

I'm sick of
dating losers

WHAT SHE REALLY MEANS

Why am I getting
dumped all the time?

Dating

WHAT SHE SAYS

I hate my ex

WHAT SHE REALLY MEANS

OMG! I still love him. I'd have him back tomorrow, but he won't have me back

Dating

WHAT SHE SAYS

Money doesn't interest me

WHAT SHE REALLY MEANS

As long as you've got enough to pay for my expensive tastes

Dating

WHAT SHE SAYS

You're a nice guy

WHAT SHE REALLY MEANS

I don't want nice. You're a wimp and I want a man

WHAT SHE SAYS

I'm not that type of girl

WHAT SHE REALLY MEANS

I so am that type of girl - just not with you

Dating

WHAT SHE SAYS

No

WHAT SHE REALLY MEANS

No

WHAT SHE SAYS

Maybe

WHAT SHE REALLY MEANS

No

Dating

WHAT SHE SAYS

Yes

WHAT SHE REALLY MEANS

Yes. But only if you get everything right. If you don't, then it's a no

Dating

WHAT SHE SAYS

I think love is more important than money

WHAT SHE REALLY MEANS

However, I DO need a huge diamond ring for our fantastic, biggest wedding ever

Dating

WHAT SHE SAYS

You'll meet someone eventually

WHAT SHE REALLY MEANS

Though probably not in this lifetime

Dating

WHAT SHE SAYS

You're the best boyfriend ever

WHAT SHE REALLY MEANS

You'll do for now

Bitching

Bitching

WHAT SHE SAYS

She's so pretty

WHAT SHE REALLY MEANS

If you like tarts with big breasts

Bitching

WHAT SHE SAYS

You really deserved that pay rise

WHAT SHE REALLY MEANS

Ass licking bitch

Bitching

WHAT SHE SAYS

You shouldn't say that about her. She's a real friend

WHAT SHE REALLY MEANS

Everything you say about her is so right. Really, you're being too kind

Bitching

WHAT SHE SAYS

She has a fabulous figure

WHAT SHE REALLY MEANS

She'd feel at home in Silicone Valley!

Bitching

WHAT SHE SAYS

You've lost weight

WHAT SHE REALLY MEANS

If you were 6 months pregnant, I'd never know it

Bitching

WHAT SHE SAYS

She's a bitch

WHAT SHE REALLY MEANS

She's better looking
than me and gets
more attention

Bitching

WHAT SHE SAYS

I wish I had your confidence

WHAT SHE REALLY MEANS

Not really. Why would I want to be an arrogant show off like you?

Bitching

WHAT SHE SAYS

No! Really? Can't believe it! You poor thing

WHAT SHE REALLY MEANS

You are confusing me with someone who gives a sh*t

Bitching

WHAT SHE SAYS

Did you see her
designer bag?

WHAT SHE REALLY MEANS

That bag is
totally fake!

Bitching

WHAT SHE SAYS

She looks good
for her age

WHAT SHE REALLY MEANS

She must have had
work done

Bitching

WHAT SHE SAYS

I haven't seen you much since you met Mark

WHAT SHE REALLY MEANS

I haven't seen you much since you ditched us for Mark

Bitching

WHAT SHE SAYS

Really? She's the same age as me?

WHAT SHE REALLY MEANS

I look a LOT younger than her

Bitching

WHAT SHE SAYS

Let's have a girls night out

WHAT SHE REALLY MEANS

My ex is out, he needs to see what he's missing

Relationships

Relationships

WHAT SHE SAYS

Don't worry about it.
Don't mention it.
It's forgotten

WHAT SHE REALLY MEANS

I'm going to
remember this for
the rest of my life

Relationships

WHAT SHE SAYS

I am NOT
over re-acting

WHAT SHE REALLY MEANS

I'm on my period

Relationships

WHAT SHE SAYS

You never listen

WHAT SHE REALLY MEANS

You never listen - EVER!

Relationships

WHAT SHE SAYS

You never listen when I'm trying to be serious

WHAT SHE REALLY MEANS

You never listen to my in-depth rants that are my perogative!

Relationships

WHAT SHE SAYS

I don't think so

WHAT SHE REALLY MEANS

Yes. But I'm not giving you full approval for what you are suggesting

Relationships

WHAT SHE SAYS

I don't think so
(said sarcastically)

WHAT SHE REALLY MEANS

Never

Relationships

WHAT SHE SAYS

Don't be ridiculous

WHAT SHE REALLY MEANS

You are ridiculous...
and stupid

Relationships

WHAT SHE SAYS

I'm not so sure

WHAT SHE REALLY MEANS

I'm absolutely certain that I do not like what you're suggesting

Relationships

WHAT SHE SAYS

Have fun on your night out

WHAT SHE REALLY MEANS

Dont you dare look at other women

Relationships

WHAT SHE SAYS

That's OK

WHAT SHE REALLY MEANS

It isn't and you are in for it

Relationships

WHAT SHE SAYS

Nothing

WHAT SHE REALLY MEANS

Something. You'll find out soon enough and you'd already know if you weren't such an idiot!

Relationships

WHAT SHE SAYS

I'm tired

WHAT SHE REALLY MEANS

You are boring me

WHAT SHE SAYS

We need to talk

WHAT SHE REALLY MEANS

You are a dead
man walking

Relationships

WHAT SHE SAYS

I'll be 5 minutes

WHAT SHE REALLY MEANS

I'll be an hour

Relationships

WHAT SHE SAYS

I'll be 10 minutes

WHAT SHE REALLY MEANS

It's your friends/family so I don't care. I'll take as long as I want

Relationships

WHAT SHE SAYS

You wouldn't like me to go out looking like this would you?

WHAT SHE REALLY MEANS

I'll be 2 hours

WHAT SHE SAYS

Don't worry. I'm fine

WHAT SHE REALLY MEANS

I'm not fine and you need to ask me what's wrong!

Relationships

WHAT SHE SAYS

I don't mind

WHAT SHE REALLY MEANS

Do what the hell you like. You'll pay later

Relationships

WHAT SHE SAYS

Do you love me?

WHAT SHE REALLY MEANS

I've bought something expensive

Relationships

WHAT SHE SAYS

I'm not in the mood

WHAT SHE REALLY MEANS

It's your fault for being the insensitive oaf that you are

Relationships

WHAT SHE SAYS

Yes, everything is perfectly alright

WHAT SHE REALLY MEANS

I just remembered something you did 7 years ago and it still annoys me when I think about it

Relationships

WHAT SHE SAYS

Do I look fat?

WHAT SHE REALLY MEANS

Tell me I look great

Relationships

WHAT SHE SAYS

I'm just popping to see my friend

WHAT SHE REALLY MEANS

I'll be gone for the rest of the day

Relationships

WHAT SHE SAYS

We'll see

WHAT SHE REALLY MEANS

No

Relationships

WHAT SHE SAYS

Yes

WHAT SHE REALLY MEANS

No

Relationships

WHAT SHE SAYS

Probably

WHAT SHE REALLY MEANS

No

Relationships

WHAT SHE SAYS

That could be
a good idea

WHAT SHE REALLY MEANS

No

Relationships

WHAT SHE SAYS

I'll think about it

WHAT SHE REALLY MEANS

No

Relationships

WHAT SHE SAYS

We're both to blame

WHAT SHE REALLY MEANS

It's all your fault

Relationships

WHAT SHE SAYS

You don't need to buy me anything

WHAT SHE REALLY MEANS

You need to buy me something VERY expensive

Relationships

WHAT SHE SAYS

I like your friends

WHAT SHE REALLY MEANS

I don't like
your friends

Relationships

WHAT SHE SAYS

I think we should move house

WHAT SHE REALLY MEANS

I want a baby

WHAT SHE SAYS

Thank you for the beautiful flowers

WHAT SHE REALLY MEANS

What have you done wrong?